SOCIAL MEDIA STRATEGY

How To Boost Your Online Presence

Ray Goodwin

CONTENTS

Title Page

Copyright

Liability Disclaimer

LIABILITY DISCLAIMER

The information contained within this book is intended for informational purposes only and should not be construed as legal or professional advice. The authors and publishers of this book are not responsible for any losses or damages that may arise from the use of the information contained within.

The reader assumes full responsibility for any decisions made based on the information in this book. The authors and publishers do not endorse any particular method, service or product mentioned in this book and are not responsible for any consequences resulting from their use.

The reader should exercise caution and discretion when making life changing decisions, and should be aware of the risks and potential consequences of their actions. This book is not a substitute for professional or legal advice and should not be relied upon as such.

By reading and using the information in this book, the reader acknowledges and agrees to hold harmless the authors, publishers, and any other parties involved in the creation or distribution of this book from any and all liability, claims, damages, or losses that may arise from their use of the information contained herein.

CHAPTER 1: UNDERSTANDING SOCIAL MEDIA STRATEGY

Hello and welcome to my latest book on the topic of Social Media. In this book, we will be delving into the world of social media strategy and how it can help you bring in more profits for your business.

As someone who has been involved in online sales for many years, I have seen the importance of social media grow exponentially. With billions of people around the world using social media platforms every day, it has become a vital tool for businesses to connect with their target audience and promote their products or services.

But simply having a presence on social media is not enough. In order to truly harness its power, you need an effective social media strategy. This involves understanding your target audience, choosing the right platforms to focus on, creating engaging content that resonates with your audience, and measuring your results so you can adjust your approach accordingly.

Throughout this book, I will share my expertise and provide practical tips on how to develop a successful social media strategy that drives sales and boosts your bottom line. So whether you are new to social media or looking to improve your existing strategy, this book is for you.

Let's get started!

Social media has become an integral part of modern day communication and marketing. As businesses continue to evolve, adapt, and thrive, it is important to understand why a social media strategy is necessary and how it can help achieve business objectives. In this chapter, we will explore the fundamentals of social media strategy and what sets it apart from social media tactics. We will also look at the elements of a successful social media strategy, common challenges in developing a strategy and ways to measure its success. Finally, we will review case studies of brands with successful social media strategies and reflect on key takeaways from this chapter.

Introduction to social media strategy

Social media sites have changed conventional marketing approaches wherein businesses can interact with their audiences in real time, engage with them, create awareness and, ultimately, convert them into loyal customers. Social Media Strategy is a structured framework that is established and implemented by a business to achieve their social media objectives. It defines the tone and style to be adopted, the way a business will engage with its target audience, the content it will produce and share, the channels it will use, and the performance metrics that will maintain and optimize its social media efforts.

Difference between social media tactics and strategy

It is important to differentiate between social media tactics and strategy. Social media tactics refer to the day-to-day execution of tactics such as creating a post, running a contest or event, managing comments, and providing customer support. Social media strategy, however, is a framework that guides these tactics, ensuring that they align with broader business goals and are executed in a way that produces optimal results.

Importance of social media strategy for businesses

Social media strategy is important for businesses because it helps in creating a roadmap to achieving marketing objectives. A well-defined social media strategy allows businesses to:

❖ Develop an effective social media presence

❖ Reach the right audience with accurate messaging

❖ Optimize costs and maximize benefits from Social Media

❖ Continuously monitor and improve social media performance in order to convert followers into customers and retain loyal customers

Elements of a successful social media strategy

A well-designed social media strategy includes the following elements:

❖ Goals and Objectives: Defining clear goals and measurable objectives for the social media campaign to align social media activities with the business objectives.

❖ Audience Segmentation: Defining target audience segments as basis for developing relevant content and tone for the targeted audience segments.

❖ Brand Identity: Defining and establishing a brand identity to project a consistent and unified messaging across all social media platforms.

❖ Content Strategy: Developing a content strategy that aligns with business objectives and target audience segments, optimizes engagement, and has a measurable impact on social media performance.

❖ Competitor Analysis: Conducting extensive research on competing brands to capture best practices, to identify gaps in communication and to ultimately gain competitive advantage.

❖ Social Media Tactics Execution Plan: Detailing the tactics and actions to be taken to implement the defined strategy.

❖ Performance Metrics and Measurement: Defining performance metrics to measure success and ensure achievement of business objectives.

Common challenges in developing a social media strategy

Developing an effective social media strategy can be a daunting task for businesses, with the following challenges often encountered:

❖ Defining clear objectives and goals - a poorly defined Social Media strategy can lead to ambiguity and lack of focus for execution.

❖ Identifying and defining the target audience - a lack of understanding or clarity around the target audience can lead to irrelevant messaging or a disconnection with the intended audience.

❖ Establishing brand identity – building a recognizable and relatable brand image among a sea of competitors can be challenging.

❖ Creating Relevant Content - generation of useful, captivating, and relevant content for social media channels to engage audience and drive conversions.

❖ Keeping pace with emerging trends - evolving social media platforms and audience behavior requires extensive effort to keep up with changing tastes.

How to measure the success of a social media strategy

Measurement of a social media strategy is critical to understand how they impact business goals and objectives. The most common metrics for measuring success include:

- ❖ Engagement rate: this is the most commonly used metric to assess what content resonates with the audience, and how they engage with the presented content.

- ❖ Reach: the audience size that is exposed to a given message post or ad.

- ❖ Acquisition Rate: metrics that measure how many users converted into paying customers or subscribers.

- ❖ Sentiment analysis: analyses the positive/negative sentiment toward the brand, product, or services in an audience.

Case studies of brands with successful social media strategies

Brands that achieved success in social media strategy show common characteristics:

- ❖ Understanding the market demand and customer segments

- ❖ Understanding the messaging that resonates with the audience

- ❖ Putting the right infrastructure in place (including distribution channels)

- ❖ Developing content strategies that engage and add value for specific target audiences

- ❖ Concentrating efforts on specific platforms comprising the target audience

Examples of brands that have established successful social media strategies include Dell, Coca-Cola, Nike, and Red Bull. Each of these brands applied sound strategy development and consistently executed it over time, creating substantial engagement from their target audience, driving conversions and retaining customer loyalty.

Key takeaways

In this chapter, we have defined the concept of social media strategy, highlighted the difference between social media tactics and strategy, and explained the importance of social media strategy for businesses. We also explored the elements of a successful social media strategy, common challenges in developing such a strategy and how to measure success. Finally, we reviewed case studies of brands that achieved success with their social media strategies. Defining a well-structured social media strategy that aligns with broader business objectives is vital for modern-day businesses to remain competitive, reach and engage with their target audience, and maximize impact from their social media investments.

CHAPTER 2: DEFINING YOUR BRAND AND AUDIENCE ON SOCIAL MEDIA

In order to create a successful social media strategy, it is essential to have a clear understanding of your brand and audience. This chapter will discuss the steps involved in defining your brand identity, identifying your target audience, creating key messaging, analyzing competitors on social media, and setting goals.

Defining brand identity:

Brand identity is all about the unique characteristics that set your brand apart from others. It includes your brand mission, values, personality, voice, and visual identity. Before you start creating content for social media, you need to have a clear understanding of your brand identity.

One way to define your brand identity is by conducting a brand audit. A brand audit is a comprehensive analysis of your brand's strengths, weaknesses, opportunities, and threats. It involves analyzing your customer base, brand perception, digital presence, and competitors.

Another way to establish your brand identity is by creating a brand style guide. A brand style guide is a document that outlines the visual and messaging standards for your brand. It establishes guidelines for the use of logos, colors, fonts, imagery, tone of voice, and writing style.

Understanding target audience:

Once you have defined your brand identity, the next step is to identify your target audience on social media. Understanding your target audience will help you create content that resonates with them and builds a connection.

To identify your target audience, you need to create buyer personas. Buyer personas are fictional representations of your ideal customers based on real data and research. They describe demographic information such as age, gender, location, education, income, job title, goals, pain points, and interests.

The key to creating effective buyer personas is to use a combination of qualitative and quantitative data. This can include customer surveys, social media analytics, website analytics, and market research.

Identifying key messaging:

Once you have a clear understanding of your brand identity and target audience, it's time to create key messaging. Key messaging is the core set of messages that you want to communicate about your brand to your target audience. It includes your brand promise, value proposition, and unique selling points.

To create effective key messaging, you need to think about what sets your brand apart from the competition. What makes your product or service unique? What problems does it solve for your target audience? Why should they choose your brand over others?

Analyzing competitors on social media:

In order to stay competitive on social media, it's important to analyze your competitors. This involves researching their social media presence, content strategy, engagement metrics, and overall brand perception.

One way to analyze your competitors is by conducting a social media audit. A social media audit is a comprehensive analysis of your competitors' social media presence. It involves analyzing their followers, engagement metrics, content strategy, and overall brand perception.

Another way to analyze your competitors is by using social media listening tools. These tools allow you to monitor mentions of your competitors on social media. Listening to what people are saying about your competitors can help you identify areas where your brand can differentiate itself.

Creating buyer personas:

Buyer personas are essential for creating a successful social media strategy. They help you understand your target audience and create content that resonates with them.

Creating buyer personas involves gathering data about your ideal customers and creating fictional representations of them. This can include demographic information such as age, gender, location, education, income, job title, goals, pain points, and interests.

It's important to use a combination of qualitative and quantitative data to create effective buyer personas. This can include customer surveys, social media analytics, website analytics, and market research.

Choosing the right social media platforms:

Once you have defined your brand identity, identified your target audience, and created key messaging, the next step is to choose the right social media platforms. Not all social media platforms are created equal, and each one has its own unique audience and features.

When choosing social media platforms, you need to consider which ones your target audience is most active on. This can be determined by looking at demographic data, engagement metrics, and survey data.

Generally speaking, Facebook is a good starting point for most brands, as it has the largest user base and a wide range of targeting options. However, it's important to consider other platforms such as Instagram, Twitter, LinkedIn, and YouTube depending on your target audience and content strategy.

Setting social media goals:

The final step in defining your brand and audience on social media is setting goals. Social media goals should be aligned with your overall business goals and should be specific, measurable, attainable, relevant, and time-bound.

Examples of social media goals include increasing brand awareness, driving website traffic, generating leads, increasing sales, and improving customer satisfaction. Once you have set your goals, you can create a social media plan that aligns with them.

Key takeaways:

Defining your brand and audience on social media is the foundation of any successful social media strategy. It involves defining your brand identity, identifying your target audience, creating key messaging, analyzing competitors on social media, choosing the right social media platforms, and setting social media goals.

To create effective buyer personas, it's important to use a

combination of qualitative and quantitative data. Social media listening tools and social media audits are also useful for analyzing competitors on social media.

Choosing the right social media platforms involves considering which ones your target audience is most active on. Social media goals should be aligned with your overall business goals and should be specific, measurable, attainable, relevant, and time-bound.

CHAPTER 3: CREATING ENGAGING CONTENT FOR SOCIAL MEDIA

Social media is a powerful tool that businesses can utilize to build relationships with their audience, generate leads, and increase sales. However, the success of a business's social media presence largely depends on how well they create and share engaging content. In this chapter, we'll cover the different types of social media content, best practices for creating and sharing content, and how to measure the effectiveness of your social media content.

Types of Social Media Content

There are many types of content that businesses can use on social media to engage their target audience. Some of the most popular types of content include:

- ❖ Images and Graphics: Images and graphics tend to be more eye-catching than plain text and can convey a message or evoke an emotion at a glance. Businesses can use high-quality images and graphics to promote their products or services, highlight customer testimonials and case studies, or showcase their team and office culture.

- ❖ Videos: Videos are an effective medium for telling stories, showcasing products or services, and providing educational content. Short videos work well on social media platforms such as Instagram, while longer videos can be shared on YouTube and Facebook.

❖ Blog Posts: Blog posts can be shared on social media platforms to drive traffic to a company's website. When writing blog posts for social media, businesses should make sure the content is interesting, engaging, and relevant to their target audience.

❖ Infographics: Infographics are a visual way to display complex information, making it easy for readers to understand. The best infographics are simple, easy-to-understand, and eye-catching.

❖ User-generated content: User-generated content (UGC) can include reviews, photos, videos, or other content created by customers or followers of a brand. UGC is a great way to showcase real-life experiences with a product or service.

Writing Effective Copy for Social Media

In addition to selecting the right type of content, businesses must also write effective copy to accompany their social media content. There are a few best practices to keep in mind when writing copy for social media:

❖ Keep it Short and Sweet: Social media is all about brevity, so businesses need to keep their copy short and to the point. Aim for one or two sentences that quickly convey the intended message and encourage engagement.

❖ Create a Compelling Headline: The headline is the first thing that users will see when scrolling through their feed, so make sure it grabs their attention. It should be clear and concise and include a call-to-action if appropriate.

❖ Use Emojis and Hashtags: Emojis and hashtags can

make copy more eye-catching and help with discoverability on social media channels. However, it's important not to overdo it and use too many.

❖ Address Your Target Audience: Social media is a space for personal connection and engagement. Addressing your target audience directly will help readers feel seen and connected to your brand.

Creating Visuals for Social Media

Visuals are essential for social media success, and there are many tools and techniques available for businesses to create high-quality visuals. Some tips for creating engaging visuals for social media include:

❖ Keep Visuals Consistent: An inconsistent visual aesthetic can lead to reduced engagement and branding confusion. When creating visual content, keep your brand guidelines in mind and ensure that your visuals align with your branding.

❖ Use High-Quality Images: High-quality visuals can instantly grab the attention of a user and make your brand look more professional.

❖ Consider Your Platform: Different social media platforms have different image size requirements. Make sure that your visuals are sized appropriately for the platform you intend to share on.

❖ Ensure Text is Legible: When using text over an image, make sure that it is easily legible on both desktop and mobile devices.

Incorporating Video into Your Social Media Content

Video content is increasingly popular on social media channels. A few tips for creating effective video content include:

❖ Keep it Short: The shorter the video, the more likely users are to watch it. Aim to keep videos between 30 seconds to two minutes in length.

❖ Use Subtitles: Many users view social media content without sound, so it's important to include subtitles or text overlays so the viewer is still able to understand the message.

❖ Embed Videos in Social Media Posts: Rather than simply sharing a link to a video, businesses should embed the video directly into their social media post. This ensures that the video thumbnail displays properly and encourages more views.

Developing a Content Calendar

Creating a content calendar is essential for consistency and staying organized. A few tips for creating a content calendar include:

❖ Identify Key Dates: Identify important dates and events such as holidays, awareness months, and product launches and ensure that these dates are included in the content calendar.

❖ Plan for Enough Lead Time: The content calendar should include enough lead time to ensure that content can be created, reviewed and approved before it is published.

❖ Allocate Enough Time for Each Platform: Each social media platform is unique, and content should be tailored appropriately for each platform. Ensure that enough time is allocated to creating content for each platform.

❖ Be Consistent: Posting regularly is essential for building an engaged audience. Keep your content calendar consistent and ensure that you are creating content on a regular basis.

Best Practices for Sharing Content on Social Media

Sharing content effectively is key to maximizing engagement. A few best practices to keep in mind when sharing content on social media include:

❖ Customize the Copy for Each Platform: Each social media platform is different, and content should be customized accordingly.

❖ Post at Optimal Times: Posting at the right time is crucial to ensuring that content is seen by the intended audience. Research the optimal posting times for each platform and schedule content accordingly.

❖ Use Hashtags: Hashtags can help with discoverability and expand the reach of your posts. Choose hashtags that are relevant to your content and your target audience.

Measuring the Effectiveness of Social Media Content

Measuring the effectiveness of social media content is essential to understand what works and what doesn't. A few ways to measure the effectiveness of social media content include:

❖ Pay Attention to Engagement Metrics: Engagement metrics, such as likes, shares, and comments, can provide valuable feedback.

❖ Track Conversions: If the goal of social media is to drive conversions, businesses should track how many conversions can directly be attributed to their social media efforts.

❖ Analyze Reach and Impressions: Reach and impressions can help businesses understand how many people their content is reaching.

❖ Stay Agile: Part of measuring the effectiveness of content is staying agile, improving on what works, and dropping what doesn't. Test new strategies and ideas and make adjustments accordingly.

Conclusion

Creating engaging content for social media is a critical part of any social media strategy. It involves using various types of content, writing effective copy, producing high-quality visuals, incorporating video, developing a content calendar, sharing content strategically, and measuring effectiveness. By following best practices for each of these areas, businesses can better engage with their audience on social media and ultimately drive more business.

CHAPTER 4: BUILDING A SOCIAL MEDIA COMMUNITY

The success of a social media strategy hinges on the ability to build a strong community. A community is defined as a group of people who share a common interest or goal. For businesses, the community is made up of customers, prospects, and other stakeholders who are interested in the brand.

Understanding Community Management on Social Media

Community management on social media is key to building a strong community. It involves interacting with community members on social media, responding to comments and messages, and moderating user-generated content.

Community management on social media should be integrated into the overall social media strategy. This involves establishing guidelines for community management, determining who will be responsible for managing the community, and setting goals for community engagement.

Responding to Comments and Messages

Responding to comments and messages is an essential part of community management on social media. It shows that the brand is listening to its audience and cares about their concerns and feedback.

When responding to comments and messages on social media, it's important to do so in a timely manner. This means responding within a few hours or a day of receiving a message or comment. This shows that the brand is actively engaged with its audience.

When responding to comments and messages, it's important to be polite and professional. Responding in a negative or defensive manner can harm the reputation of the brand. It's also important to address the concerns or questions of the community member in a thorough and thoughtful manner.

Creating a Social Media Content Feedback Loop

A social media content feedback loop involves using feedback from the community to inform content creation. This involves monitoring social media channels for feedback from the community, analyzing the feedback, and using it to inform future content creation.

The feedback loop should be built into the overall social media strategy. This involves defining the process for collecting and analyzing feedback, determining who will be responsible for managing the feedback loop, and setting goals for using feedback to inform content creation.

Moderating User-Generated Content

Moderating user-generated content is an important part of community management on social media. User-generated content can be a powerful tool for building community engagement, but it can also be a source of negative feedback and criticism.

When moderating user-generated content, it's important to establish guidelines for what is allowed and what is not allowed. This involves setting clear guidelines for what types of content are appropriate for the brand and what types of content are not.

Handling Negative Feedback on Social Media

Negative feedback is inevitable on social media. It's important to handle negative feedback in a way that is professional and respectful.

When handling negative feedback on social media, it's important to respond in a timely manner. This shows that the brand is actively engaged with its audience and cares about their concerns.

It's also important to respond to negative feedback in a way that is professional and respectful. Responding in a negative or defensive manner can harm the reputation of the brand.

Encouraging User Engagement through Contests and Giveaways

Contests and giveaways are an effective way to encourage user engagement on social media. This involves offering prizes or incentives to community members who participate in the contest or giveaway.

When creating a contest or giveaway on social media, it's important to establish clear guidelines for participation. This involves defining the rules of the contest or giveaway, determining the prize or incentive, and setting a deadline for participation.

Cultivating Brand Ambassadors on Social Media

Brand ambassadors are community members who are passionate about the brand and help promote it on social media. Cultivating brand ambassadors is an important part of community management on social media.

When cultivating brand ambassadors on social media, it's important to identify community members who are passionate about the brand and have a large following on social media. This involves monitoring social media channels for community members who are actively promoting the brand and engaging with them on social media.

Once brand ambassadors are identified, it's important to nurture the relationship by providing them with exclusive content, access to events, and other incentives that show the brand's appreciation for their support.

Key Takeaways

Building a social media community is crucial to the success of a social media strategy. This involves community management on social media, responding to comments and messages, moderating user-generated content, handling negative feedback on social media, encouraging user engagement through contests and giveaways, and cultivating brand ambassadors on social media. By building a strong community, brands can increase engagement, loyalty, and ultimately, sales.

CHAPTER 5: LEVERAGING INFLUENCERS FOR YOUR SOCIAL MEDIA STRATEGY

Influencer marketing is one of the most effective ways to increase brand awareness, drive engagement, and boost conversions on social media. Brands can harness the power of influencers to reach a wider audience, build credibility, and establish trust with their target demographic. However, finding the right influencers and creating a successful influencer campaign can be challenging. In this chapter, we will explore the key steps in leveraging influencers for your social media strategy.

Understanding Influencer Marketing

Influencer marketing involves partnering with individuals who have a large following on social media to promote your brand or product to their followers. Influencers can be celebrities, industry experts, bloggers, or social media personalities who have a significant following and a high level of engagement with their audience. Brands can leverage influencers to reach a wider audience that is already interested in their niche or industry.

Finding the Right Influencers for Your Brand

To find the right influencers for your brand, you need to consider several factors. First, your ideal influencer should have a large following that is relevant to your brand and niche. They should also have a high level of engagement with their followers, demonstrated by likes, comments, shares, and other interactions. You should also look for influencers whose values align with your brand, who have a positive reputation, and who have a significant impact on their followers' purchasing decisions.

There are various tools available to help you find the right influencers for your brand. You can use social media listening tools to identify relevant conversations and hashtags within your niche. You can also use influencer discovery platforms like Upfluence, AspireIQ, and Fohr to find relevant influencers and track their performance.

Negotiating Partnerships with Influencers

Once you have identified potential influencers for your brand, you need to negotiate a partnership that benefits both parties. You need to define the scope of the partnership, the deliverables, and the compensation. The compensation will depend on the influencer's profile, the scope of work, and the length of the campaign. The compensation can take the form of a fee, free products or services, or a combination of both.

Creating a Successful Influencer Campaign

To create a successful influencer campaign, you need to define clear campaign objectives, ensure that the influencer's content aligns with your brand's values and messaging, and provide creative freedom to the influencer. You also need to establish clear guidelines for compliance and disclosure. Compliance guidelines ensure that the influencer follows the advertising guidelines of the social media platform and complies with the Federal Trade Commission's (FTC) endorsement guidelines. Disclosure guidelines ensure that the influencer discloses their partnership with your brand.

Measuring the ROI of Influencer Marketing

To measure the ROI of influencer marketing, you need to establish clear campaign objectives and track key metrics. These metrics can include engagement rate, reach, impressions, conversions, sales, and return on ad spend (ROAS). You can use social media analytics tools like Hootsuite, Sprout Social, or Socialbakers to track your campaign's performance.

Avoiding Common Pitfalls in Influencer Marketing

One common pitfall in influencer marketing is partnering with influencers who have fake followers or low engagement rates. You should also avoid partnering with influencers who have a negative reputation or whose values do not align with your brand.

Leveraging Micro-Influencers for Your Brand

Micro-influencers are individuals who have a smaller following than macro-influencers but have a high level of engagement with their audience. Micro-influencers can be more affordable than macro-influencers and can have a more niche and loyal following. Brands can leverage micro-influencers to reach a more targeted audience and build engagement.

Key Takeaways:

❖ Influencer marketing can help brands reach a wider audience, build credibility, and establish trust with their target demographic.

❖ Brands should find influencers whose values align with

their brand, who have a positive reputation, and who have a significant impact on their followers' purchasing decisions.

❖   A successful influencer campaign involves defining clear campaign objectives, ensuring that the influencer's content aligns with the brand's values and messaging, and establishing clear guidelines for compliance and disclosure.

❖   Brands can measure the ROI of influencer marketing by tracking key metrics such as engagement rate, reach, impressions, conversions, sales, and ROAS.

❖   Brands should avoid partnering with influencers who have fake followers, low engagement rates, a negative reputation, or whose values do not align with their brand.

❖   Micro-influencers can be more affordable and can have a more niche and loyal following than macro-influencers.

CHAPTER 6: INTEGRATING SOCIAL MEDIA INTO YOUR MARKETING MIX

Social media has become a powerful tool for businesses to connect with customers, build brand awareness, and drive sales. While implementing a social media strategy can be complex, the key is to integrate social media into your marketing mix to maximize its impact. In this chapter, we will discuss the role of social media in the marketing mix, aligning social media strategy with overall marketing goals, incorporating social media into traditional marketing efforts, and creating a social media crisis management plan.

The Role of Social Media in the Marketing Mix

Marketing mix refers to a company's overall marketing strategy. It includes the four Ps – product, price, promotion, and place. The marketing mix is a framework that helps businesses define their marketing strategy and implement it effectively. Social media has become an integral part of the marketing mix, and it can be used to address each of the four Ps effectively.

❖ Product: Social media can be used to showcase products and services. Businesses can use social media to showcase their products and services through creative content and engage customers in a conversation about how their offerings can meet their needs.

❖ Price: Social media can be used to promote special offers, discounts, and promotions. Announcing exclusive discounts or offering incentives to customers who follow their social media channels can help drive sales.

❖ Promotion: Social media can be used to create brand awareness. It provides businesses with the opportunity to reach out to a wider audience and build a community around their brand.

❖ Place: Social media can also be used to reach customers where they are. By creating a social media presence, businesses can engage with customers on their terms.

Aligning Your Social Media Strategy with Overall Marketing Goals

The success of your social media strategy largely depends on how well it aligns with your overall marketing goals. To create an effective, integrated social media strategy, businesses need to ensure their social media efforts align with other marketing channels such as email, search engine optimization (SEO), and events.

First, identify your business's overall marketing goals, such as increasing sales, building brand awareness, or expanding market share. Next, identify how social media can help achieve these goals. For example, if your goal is to increase sales, social media can be used to promote special offers, discounts, and promotions to your audience.

With clear goals in mind, businesses can then identify which social media platforms are best suited to achieving these goals. By knowing your audience, businesses can ensure their content is shared on platforms where their target audience is most active.

Incorporating Social Media into Traditional Marketing Efforts

Beyond the online realm, social media can also be used to drive traffic to offline marketing campaigns. By creating hashtags, businesses can encourage customers to share their experiences at events, effectively amplifying the reach of the event. Social media can also be used to promote webinars, conferences, or other events by sharing registration details and key speakers.

While social media is an effective marketing tool, it can't be relied upon in isolation. Social media must be integrated with other marketing channels to achieve the desired impact.

Creating a Social Media Crisis Management Plan

One of the challenges of social media marketing is managing a potential crisis that can arise from use of this channel. It is important to have a crisis management plan in place to effectively manage any crisis that may arise.

First, create a social media response team and train them on how to respond to different kinds of social media problems. This team should be made up of employees from different departments including communications, marketing, and customer service. Establish who has the authority to respond in real-time and what communication methods will be used.

Second, establish a workflow for responding to negative social media feedback. This workflow could include a set of pre-written, approved messages specific to each type of feedback that can be adapted and used when necessary.

Third, monitor social media mentions and track key metrics to measure the impact of the crisis on the business. Establish tools to actively monitor social media channels for mentions of the business and key competitors.

Fourth, respond to negative feedback or address a crisis promptly. What the response should be will depend on the situation, and it is best handled by professionals who are trained to manage crises and respond positively.

Finally, conduct an analysis post-crisis to identify lessons learned. Analyze and document how the social media crisis was handled, what can be improved and how the business can implement changes to prevent similar problems from recurring in the future.

Conclusion

Integrating social media into the marketing mix is essential for businesses looking to leverage the power of social media effectively. By aligning social media strategies with overall marketing goals, businesses can create integrated campaigns across channels that drive engagement, build awareness, and drive sales. Incorporating social media into traditional marketing efforts and having a crisis management plan in place allows businesses to navigate any potential challenges deftly, minimizing damage. By constantly analyzing and tweaking efforts, your business can extract maximum value from social media, drive effective engagement, and stay ahead of the competition.

CHAPTER 7: MAXIMIZING PAID ADVERTISING ON SOCIAL MEDIA

Social media advertising has become an essential part of the marketing mix for businesses of all sizes and industries. With the rise in algorithms and changes to organic reach, it's important to consider investing in paid advertising to maximize your social media strategy. Paid advertising allows you to reach a larger audience, target specific demographics, and track engagement metrics to help improve your overall social media strategy.

Understanding the Different Types of Social Media Advertising

Social media advertising comes in many forms and can be adapted to fit different marketing goals. Here are a few types of social media advertising:

❖ Sponsored posts: These are native ads that appear within a user's newsfeed in a seamless way. It's important to make sure that your sponsored posts are clearly marked as ads, so your audience is aware of the promotion. Sponsored posts can either be in the form of static images or videos.

❖ Display ads: Display ads are traditional banner ads that appear on the sidebar or top/bottom of a website, app, or social media platform.

❖ Instagram Stories: Instagram Stories are short video or image slideshows that give advertisers an opportunity to promote their product or service in an engaging way.

❖ Influencer marketing: Collaborating with influencers can be an effective way to reach a specific target audience and gain credibility through the influencer's audience.

Setting Up a Social Media Advertising Campaign

Before launching any social media advertising campaign, it's important to establish clear goals and objectives. These goals can include increasing brand awareness, driving sales, or boosting engagement. Here are some steps to follow when setting up a social media advertising campaign:

❖ Choose the right platform(s): It's important to choose the social media platform(s) that align with your target audience. It's important to conduct research to see which platforms your audience is most active on.

❖ Define your target audience: Once you've chosen the platform(s), you need to define your target audience. This includes age, location, interests, behaviors, and more. The more details you can gather, the more targeted your campaign can be.

❖ Create unique and compelling ad content: Your social media ad needs to capture the attention of your audience and leave an impression. Try to create visuals and copy that connect emotionally with your audience.

❖ Set a budget and bid strategy: Social media advertising can quickly become expensive if you don't set a budget. Determine how much you're willing to spend and use an optimized bid strategy to ensure your money is being spent effectively.

❖ Launch and monitor the campaign: Once your campaign is launched, continually monitor engagement metrics to track effectiveness. Adjust the campaign settings if need be.

Measuring the Success of Social Media Advertising Campaigns

It's crucial to measure the success of your social media advertising campaigns to determine if they are aligned with your business goals. Key metrics to track include cost-per-click (CPC), click-through-rate (CTR), engagement, conversions, and return on investment (ROI). Additionally, it's important to measure key demographics such as age, gender, and location to fine-tune your targeting.

Best Practices for Optimizing Social Media Advertising

To truly maximize the results of your social media advertising strategy, here are some best practices to follow:

1. Create a sense of urgency: Use language in your ad copy that creates a sense of urgency to drive immediate action from your audience. Offer limited time discounts or promotions to create a sense of urgency.

2. Test multiple ad formats: Test different ad formats, such as static images versus videos, to see what resonates most with your audience.

3. Use retargeting: Retargeting allows you to build an audience from users who have interacted with your brand online. You can then create a personalized ad campaign targeting this specific audience.

4. Don't ignore small audiences: Small audiences can generate important data that can inform your target audience and messaging for future campaigns. Small audiences can also provide

valuable leads that could translate into high-value customers going forward.

5. Continually optimize: Continually analyze the metrics of your social media advertising campaigns and utilize the data to make targeted adjustments and optimizations.

Key Takeaways

Social media advertising is an essential part of any social media strategy. It allows businesses to reach a wider audience and provide targeted advertisements to their ideal customer base. Social media advertising comes in many different forms including sponsored posts, display ads, Instagram stories, and influencer marketing. Before launching any social media advertising campaign, it's important to establish clear goals and objectives, and monitor engagement metrics to track effectiveness. To truly maximize the results of your social media advertising strategy, continuously optimize ad content and target audience.

CHAPTER 8:
ANALYZING SOCIAL MEDIA METRICS

Social media analytics is essential in measuring the effectiveness of your social media strategy. In this chapter, we will discuss the importance of social media metrics, identifying key performance indicators (KPIs), measuring social media engagement, analyzing social media reach and impressions, determining the ROI of social media marketing, using social media metrics to improve your strategy, and key takeaways.

Understanding Social Media Analytics

Social media analytics refers to the process of tracking, analyzing, and interpreting data from social media platforms. It enables businesses to understand their social media performance and determine which strategies are most effective in achieving their social media goals.

Social media analytics involves tracking several metrics, including engagement, reach, impressions, and conversion rates. These metrics help businesses to evaluate their social media performance and adjust their strategies accordingly.

Identifying Key Performance Indicators (KPIs)

Key performance indicators (KPIs) are specific metrics that are used to evaluate the success of a social media strategy. KPIs will vary depending on the goals of your social media strategy. For example, if your goal is to increase brand awareness, your KPIs might include reach, impressions, and engagement.

If your goal is to increase website traffic, you might track click-through rates, referral traffic, and bounce rates. When selecting KPIs, it is essential to ensure that they are specific, measurable, and aligned with your social media goals.

Measuring Social Media Engagement

Social media engagement refers to the level of interaction a user has with your content. It can be measured using metrics such as likes, comments, shares, and clicks. High levels of engagement are an indication that your content is resonating well with your audience.

To improve engagement, businesses need to create content that is informative, entertaining, or valuable to their audience. Additionally, providing a call-to-action (CTA) can encourage engagement by prompting users to take further action, such as commenting or sharing a post.

Analyzing Social Media Reach and Impressions

Social media reach is the number of unique users that have seen your post, while impressions refer to the total number of times your post has been displayed. Both metrics are essential in evaluating your social media strategy and identifying the content that resonates with your audience

Businesses can improve their reach and impressions by creating engaging content, incorporating visuals and videos into their posts, and using paid advertising to increase their overall reach.

Determining the ROI of Social Media Marketing

Return on investment (ROI) is essential in evaluating the financial success of your social media strategy. To measure social media ROI, businesses need to track sales and revenue generated through social media channels compared to the cost of running their social media campaigns.

While measuring social media ROI can be challenging, understanding your return on investment is essential to determine which social media strategies are most effective in driving revenue.

Using Social Media Metrics to Improve Your Strategy

Social media metrics play a vital role in improving a business's social media strategy. By analyzing your social media performance, you can adjust your social media strategy to increase your reach, engagement, and ROI.

For example, if you notice that your engagement rates are low, you might experiment with different types of content to see which resonates well with your audience. If your reach is low, you might consider running paid advertising to extend your reach.

Using social media metrics is a continuous process that requires constant monitoring and adjustment. By analyzing your social media metrics regularly, you can continue to optimize your social media strategy for success.

Key Takeaways

- ❖ Social media analytics refers to tracking, analyzing, and interpreting data from social media platforms.

- ❖ Key performance indicators (KPIs) are specific metrics used to evaluate the success of your social media strategy.

- ❖ Measuring social media engagement is essential in determining whether your content resonates well with your audience.

❖ Analyzing social media reach and impressions can help businesses identify the content that resonates best with their audience.

❖ Measuring the ROI of social media marketing is essential to determine which social media strategies are effective in driving revenue.

❖ Using social media metrics to improve your strategy is a continuous process that requires constant monitoring and adjustment.

CHAPTER 9: STAYING AHEAD OF SOCIAL MEDIA TRENDS

In the constantly evolving world of social media, staying up-to-date with the latest trends is crucial to being successful. In this chapter, we will discuss the strategies and techniques you can use to stay ahead of social media trends.

Following Industry Thought Leaders

One of the best ways to stay informed about the latest trends in social media is to follow industry thought leaders on social media platforms such as Twitter, LinkedIn, and Facebook. By following the right people, you can stay up-to-date with the latest news, trends, and best practices in social media.

To find relevant thought leaders to follow, you can search for industry experts and influencers on social media platforms and follow their accounts. You can also search for relevant hashtags and participate in social media conversations to discover new thought leaders and connect with other industry professionals.

Keeping Up with the Latest Social Media Updates and Changes

Social media platforms are constantly updating their algorithms and adding new features to their platforms. It is important to keep up with these changes so that you can adapt your social media strategy accordingly.

One way to stay updated with the latest social media updates and changes is to subscribe to industry newsletters and blogs. These sources provide regular updates on social media news, trends, and changes, allowing you to stay informed without having to constantly monitor social media platforms.

Monitoring Social Media Trends

Monitoring social media trends is an important part of staying ahead of the curve. By tracking trends on social media platforms, you can identify upcoming trends and adapt your social media strategy accordingly.

To monitor social media trends, you can use social media monitoring tools such as Hootsuite, Sprout Social, and Brandwatch. These tools allow you to monitor social media conversations and hashtags and track mentions of your brand, competitors, and industry keywords.

Forecasting Social Media Trends

Forecasting social media trends is another important aspect of staying ahead of the curve. By predicting upcoming trends, you can adjust your social media strategy to capitalize on these trends before they become mainstream.

To forecast social media trends, you can use a variety of sources such as social media monitoring tools, industry reports, and expert opinions. By analyzing these sources, you can identify patterns and emerging trends, allowing you to adjust your social media strategy accordingly.

Incorporating Emerging Trends into Your Social Media Strategy

Once you have identified upcoming social media trends, it is important to incorporate them into your social media strategy. By staying ahead of the curve, you can differentiate your brand from competitors and reach new audiences.

To incorporate emerging trends into your social media strategy, you can experiment with new content formats such as video, podcasts, and live streams. You can also participate in social media challenges and hashtags that align with your brand values and attract your target audience.

Experimenting with New Social Media Features

Social media platforms are constantly adding new features and formats that can help you reach new audiences and engage with your followers. By experimenting with new social media features, you can stay ahead of the curve and differentiate your brand from competitors.

To experiment with new social media features, you can keep an eye out for platform updates and new feature announcements on social media blogs and websites. You can also participate in social media betas and experiments to get early access to new features and provide feedback to platform developers.

Conclusion

Staying ahead of social media trends is crucial to being successful in the constantly evolving landscape of social media. By following industry thought leaders, keeping up with the latest social media updates and changes, monitoring social media trends, forecasting upcoming trends, incorporating emerging trends into your social media strategy, and experimenting with new social media features, you can stay ahead of the curve and differentiate your brand from competitors.

CHAPTER 10: INTEGRATING EMPLOYEE ADVOCACY INTO YOUR SOCIAL MEDIA STRATEGY

Social media is no longer just the responsibility of the marketing department. Companies have realized that their employees are their best brand ambassadors and that they have a critical role to play in their social media strategy. When an employee shares their company's content or talks about their experience working with the company, they're more likely to be seen as trustworthy by their peers.

In this chapter, we'll explore how to integrate employee advocacy into your social media strategy. We'll discuss why employee advocacy is important, how to encourage employee advocacy, and how to measure the impact of employee advocacy on social media.

Understanding Employee Advocacy

Employee advocacy is the promotion of a company's products, services, or brand by its employees. Employee advocacy is not about forcing employees to share company content on their personal social media profiles. Instead, it's about empowering employees to become brand ambassadors.

When employees share company content on their social media profiles, they're able to reach a wider audience than the company would be able to reach on its own. This is because the employees have built up their own networks of followers who trust them and are more likely to engage with the content they share.

Empowering employees as brand ambassadors is a win-win situation for both employers and employees. Employees feel more connected to their company and are more likely to stay long term, while the company benefits from increased brand recognition and engagement.

Encouraging Employee Advocacy

Encouraging employee advocacy requires more than sending occasional emails reminding employees to share company content on social media. Instead, it requires a well-crafted plan that includes training, incentives, and ongoing support.

Here are some best practices for encouraging employee advocacy:

❖ Define your goals: Before you can encourage employee advocacy, you need to define your goals. Are you looking to increase brand awareness, drive traffic to your website, or generate sales? Once you have a clear goal, you can start to develop a plan to encourage employee advocacy.

❖ Train your employees: Not all employees will be comfortable with sharing company content on social media. It's important to provide training to ensure they understand the company's social media policies, the appropriate use of hashtags, and how to measure the impact of their social media activities.

❖ Provide content: Make it easy for employees to share content on social media. Provide them with a mix of company-related content, industry news, and content that helps them build their personal brand.

❖   Create incentives: Consider creating incentives for employees who share company content on social media. This could include recognition, prizes, or even financial incentives.

❖   Share success stories: Celebrate the success of employee advocacy by sharing success stories. Highlight employees who have successfully promoted the company through their social media channels. This will help inspire other employees to become brand ambassadors.

Measuring the Impact of Employee Advocacy

Measuring the impact of employee advocacy on social media can be challenging, but it's important to measure to understand the success of your program. Here are some key metrics to consider:

❖   Engagement: Measure the engagement your content receives when shared by employees versus when shared by the company. Are there differences in the number of likes, shares, and comments?

❖   Reach: Measure the total number of people reached when content is shared by employees versus when shared by the company. This will help you determine how much additional reach your employee advocacy program is providing.

❖   Conversions: If your goal is to generate sales, you'll want to measure how many conversions come from content shared by employees versus content shared by the company.

❖   Employee Participation: Measure the number of employees who are participating in the employee advocacy program. Are there any employees who have a higher impact than others?

Overcoming Common Challenges in Employee Advocacy

Implementing an employee advocacy program can be challenging. Here are some common challenges and how to overcome them:

❖   Lack of employee interest: Some employees may not want to participate in an employee advocacy program. To overcome this, consider providing incentives and highlighting the benefits of employee advocacy.

❖   Fear of negative feedback: Some employees may worry about receiving negative feedback on social media. To overcome this, provide training and guidelines for responding to negative feedback.

❖   Limited reach: Some employees may have limited social media reach. To overcome this, provide content that employees can share with their offline networks, such as email newsletters or printed materials.

❖   Inconsistency: Employees may share content on social media inconsistently, making it difficult to measure the impact of the program. To overcome this, create a calendar of content and encourage employees to share regularly.

Key Takeaways

In this chapter, we explored the importance of integrating employee advocacy into your social media strategy. We discussed the benefits of employee advocacy, best practices for encouraging employee advocacy, how to measure the impact of employee advocacy, and how to overcome common challenges.

As companies continue to recognize the value of employee advocacy on social media, it's important to develop a plan that is well-crafted and ongoing. By empowering employees as brand ambassadors, companies can increase their reach, engage with their audience, and build a positive reputation.

CHAPTER 11: DEVELOPING A SOCIAL MEDIA POLICY

In today's digital age, having a strong social media policy is more important than ever before. A social media policy provides guidance and boundaries for employees to follow when using social media on behalf of the company. In this chapter, we will outline the key elements of a social media policy and provide guidance on how to create and enforce one.

Understanding the Importance of a Social Media Policy

A social media policy is essential for any company that has a presence on social media. It helps ensure that employees are representing the company in a professional manner and that they are not sharing confidential information or making statements that could damage the company's reputation. A social media policy also outlines the consequences of violating company guidelines and provides employees with the tools they need to be successful social media ambassadors for the brand.

Creating a Social Media Policy for Your Organization

When creating a social media policy, it's important to keep in mind that the rules and regulations can vary depending on the industry and the company's culture. A social media policy should also be updated regularly to reflect any changes in social media trends, platform policies, or company guidelines.

To create a social media policy, start by identifying what types of information can be shared and what should be kept private. It's important to clearly define what constitutes confidential information and ensure that all employees know what they can and cannot share on social media.

The policy should also establish a tone and style that is in line with the company's brand. This means establishing guidelines for the use of language, tone, and grammar. It's important to provide clear guidance on how employees can and should represent the company on social media platforms.

Communicating the Social Media Policy to Employees

Once a social media policy has been written, it's important to communicate it to all employees. This can be done through a variety of channels, including email, team meetings, or a dedicated section on the company intranet. It is also important to ensure that new employees are educated on the policy during onboarding.

Enforcing the Social Media Policy

Enforcement of the social media policy is essential to ensure that employees are following the guidelines outlined in the policy. This can be done through regular monitoring of social media accounts, training sessions, and reminders via email or other forms of communication.

Updating the Social Media Policy as Needed

As social media platforms and trends evolve, it's important to regularly review and update the social media policy to keep it up to date. This may involve adding new guidelines or revising existing guidelines to keep pace with changes in technology or trends.

Handling Social Media Policy Violations

If an employee violates the social media policy, it's important to take corrective action. Depending on the severity of the violation, this could include a warning, suspension, or termination. It's important to enforce the policy consistently to ensure that employees understand the importance of following company guidelines on social media.

Key Takeaways

- ❖ A social media policy is essential for any company that has a presence on social media.

- ❖ A social media policy should be updated regularly to reflect changes in social media trends, platform policies, or company guidelines.

- ❖ A social media policy should clearly define what information can be shared and what should be kept confidential.

- ❖ The policy should establish a tone and style that is in line with the company's brand.

- ❖ It's important to communicate the social media policy to all employees and ensure that new employees are educated on the policy.

- ❖ Enforcement of the social media policy is essential to ensure that employees are following the guidelines outlined in the policy.

- ❖ If an employee violates the social media policy, corrective action should be taken to ensure that the employee understands the importance of following company guidelines on social media.

In conclusion, a social media policy is an essential component of any successful social media strategy. It provides employees with clear guidelines on how to represent the company on social media platforms and ensures that confidential company information is kept private. By creating and enforcing a social media policy, companies can mitigate potential risks and unleash the power of social media to help grow their business.

CHAPTER 12: MANAGING YOUR SOCIAL MEDIA REPUTATION

In the digital age, reputation management is essential, and social media plays a significant role in shaping a brand's reputation. Social media platforms give individuals and businesses a voice, allowing them to share their thoughts and opinions with the world in a matter of seconds. This can be both beneficial and detrimental to a brand's reputation.

In this chapter, we will discuss the importance of managing your social media reputation and the steps you can take to protect it.

Understanding the impact of reputation on social media

Your brand's reputation is everything. It's what sets you apart from your competitors and builds trust among your customers. In today's world, social media is the primary source of information for many consumers, and how they perceive your brand on social media can have a significant impact on your business.

Negative comments, reviews, or feedback on social media can harm your brand's reputation and discourage potential customers. On the other hand, positive feedback can generate buzz, attract new customers, and improve your brand image.

Monitoring your brand's online reputation

The first step in managing your social media reputation is to monitor what people are saying about your brand. There are several tools that you can use to monitor your brand's online presence, including:

❖ Google Alerts: Set up Google Alerts to be notified whenever your brand is mentioned online.

❖ Social media monitoring tools: There are several social media monitoring tools available, such as Hootsuite Insights, Mention, and Sprout Social.

❖ Native platform insights: Most social media platforms offer insights and analytics that can help you monitor your brand's activity on their platform.

Responding to negative feedback on social media

Ignoring negative feedback on social media can be damaging to your brand's reputation. When someone leaves a negative comment or review on your social media profiles, respond quickly and professionally. Here are a few tips for responding to negative feedback on social media:

1. Address the issue: Acknowledge the customer's concerns and address the issue at hand. Apologize if necessary and offer a solution or plan to resolve the issue.

2. Be respectful: Respond to negative feedback in a respectful and professional manner. Avoid getting defensive or confrontational.

3. Move the conversation offline: If possible, move the conversation offline to a phone call or email. This can help diffuse the situation and prevent negative feedback from escalating.

Creating a crisis management plan for social media

In today's fast-paced digital world, it's important to have a crisis management plan in place to anticipate and respond to negative feedback or any potential reputation-damaging events. Here are a few steps you can take to create a crisis management plan for social media:

❖ Identify potential crises: Brainstorm potential situations that could negatively impact your brand's reputation on social media and plan for them accordingly.

❖ Create a response plan: Develop a plan for responding to negative feedback on social media. Identify who will be responsible for responding, what they will say, and how they will handle the situation.

❖ Define messaging: Define the messaging you'll use to address a crisis, including talking points and tone of voice.

❖ Set up a communication protocol: Establish a communication protocol among your team for sharing information and updates during a crisis.

Preventing reputation damage on social media

Preventing reputation damage is always better than managing it after the fact. Here are a few steps you can take to prevent reputation damage on social media:

❖ Set up alerts: Set up alerts to help you stay informed about any online mentions of your brand, so you can address issues as soon as they arise.

❖ Respond to all comments: Responding to all comments can help build goodwill among your audience. Make sure you're responding in a timely and professional manner.

❖ Stay on top of trends: Stay tuned to social media trends and keep your content and strategy relevant to engage and entertain your audience.

Building a positive reputation on social media

To build a positive reputation on social media, you need to be proactive with your strategy. Here are a few tips to help you build a positive reputation:

❖ Post engaging content: Create and share content that is valuable, relevant, and engaging to your audience.

❖ Build relationships: Focus on building relationships with your audience by responding to comments, re-sharing user-generated content, and engaging in conversations.

❖ Share positive feedback: Share positive feedback on your social media channels to reinforce your brand's positive reputation.

In conclusion, social media can be a valuable tool for building your brand's reputation, but it can also have a significant impact on your reputation if not managed properly. To protect your brand's reputation, you need to monitor your online presence, respond to negative feedback professionally, and be proactive in building a positive reputation. By doing so, you can ensure that your brand's online image accurately reflects your business values, mission, and goals.

CHAPTER 13: SCALING YOUR SOCIAL MEDIA STRATEGY

Scaling your social media strategy can be challenging due to the ever-evolving nature of social media. However, successful scaling is essential if you want to see real growth. Scaling your social media strategy means creating processes and procedures that allow you to increase your audience reach, engagement, and revenue generation while managing the demands of a larger audience.

Understanding the challenges of scaling a social media strategy is crucial. Some of the key challenges include an increase in message volume, managing a larger audience, and the need for greater levels of automation. Fortunately, these challenges can be overcome with effective planning and implementation.

Creating processes for scaling your social media efforts involves identifying roles and responsibilities and putting systems in place to manage them effectively. This requires the creation of a social media style guide, scheduling tools, and a process for monitoring and responding to inquiries.

Leveraging automation is another essential aspect of scaling your social media strategy. There are many tools available that allow you to automate processes such as social media scheduling and posting, content curation, and analytics tracking. These tools can save you time and help you to maintain the quality of your content. However, it is important to balance automation with genuine engagement to avoid appearing robotic and disingenuous.

Delegating social media responsibilities is one of the cornerstones of successful scaling. By assigning specific roles and responsibilities, you can create a clear and efficient process for managing your social media accounts. This may involve hiring additional staff, outsourcing to freelancers, or bringing on interns. Regardless of the approach, clearly define roles and expectations to ensure seamless collaboration.

Measuring the effectiveness of your scaled social media efforts is critical to determining whether you are achieving your objectives. Metrics to monitor may include increased followers, engagement, clicks, and website traffic. By tracking these metrics, you can course-correct as necessary and optimize your social media strategy for even greater success.

Best practices for scaling a social media strategy include prioritizing customer insights, focusing on quality over quantity, and staying up-to-date on social media trends. Incorporating key lessons and strategies from other successful brands can also be a valuable tool in helping you refine your approach.

In conclusion, scaling your social media strategy may seem daunting, but with careful planning, it is achievable. By understanding the challenges of scaling, creating processes, leveraging automation, delegating responsibilities, measuring effectiveness, and following best practices, you can effectively grow your social media presence, build a larger audience base, and take your business to the next level.

CHAPTER 14: DEVELOPING A SOCIAL MEDIA PLAN FOR EVENTS

Events are an integral part of any marketing strategy, and social media has the power to take event marketing to the next level. Social media can help you promote your event, engage attendees, and even drive ticket sales. In this chapter, we'll look at the steps you need to take to develop a social media plan for events.

Understanding the Role of Social Media in Event Marketing

Social media is an important marketing tool for events as it is an effective way to connect with your target audience before, during, and after the event. With social media, you can:

❖ Share event information and updates with attendees and potential attendees

❖ Encourage attendees to engage with your brand and event

❖ Promote your event to a wider audience

❖ Generate buzz and excitement around your event

❖ Drive ticket sales

❖ Use user-generated content to showcase the event to a

wider audience

Creating a Social Media Plan for Events

Developing a social media plan for events is essential to ensure that your social media efforts are aligned with your overall event marketing strategy. Here are the steps involved in creating an effective social media plan for events:

1. Set Social Media Goals

Before developing a social media plan for events, it is important to understand what you want to achieve from your social media efforts. Your goals should be specific, measurable, achievable, relevant, and time-bound (SMART). Some common goals for events could be to:

❖ Increase ticket sales

❖ Boost attendance

❖ Drive social media engagement and shares

❖ Increase brand awareness

2. Identify Your Target Audience

Knowing your target audience is crucial to developing an effective social media plan for events. You need to know who your audience is, what social media platforms they use, and what type of content appeals to them. Creating personas is one way to identify your target audience.

3. Choose the Right Social Media Platforms

Based on your target audience, choose the social media platforms that are a good fit for your event. For example, if your event targets a younger demographic, you may want to focus on platforms such as Instagram and Snapchat. Each platform has its unique strengths, and you need to choose the ones that align with your goals and audience.

4. Create a Content Plan

Once you have identified your social media platforms, you need to create a content plan for each platform. Your content should be engaging, informative, and relevant to your audience. Some common types of content that work well for events include:

❖ Event teasers and announcement videos

❖ Behind-the-scenes content

❖ Live videos from the event

❖ Contest and giveaways to engage attendees

❖ User-generated content from attendees

5. Promote Your Event on Social Media

Social media is a powerful tool to promote your event and drive ticket sales. Here are some ways to promote your event on social media:

❖ Create event-specific hashtags and encourage attendees to use them

❖ Share event teasers and announcements on social media

❖ Use targeted social media advertising to reach potential attendees

❖ Offer exclusive social media promotions and discounts for ticket sales

6. Encourage Attendees to Engage on Social Media During the Event

Encouraging attendees to engage with your event on social media can help generate buzz and engagement. Here are some ways to encourage attendees to engage on social media during your event:

❖ Use social display screens to showcase social media posts from attendees

❖ Create social media contests and giveaways for attendees

❖ Use live social media polls and Q&A sessions during the event

❖ Encourage attendees to share their event experience on social media using a branded hashtag

7. Use User-generated Content to Showcase the Event

User-generated content can be a powerful way to showcase your event to a wider audience. Encourage attendees to use your event hashtag and share their experience on social media. You can curate this content and use it in your event recap videos, social media posts, and even your website.

Measuring the Impact of Social Media on Event Success

Measuring the impact of your social media efforts is crucial to understanding the effectiveness of your social media plan for events. Here are some metrics you can track:

❖ Ticket sales from social media promotions

❖ Attendance numbers

❖ Social media engagement levels

- ❖ Number of social media followers

- ❖ Number of shares, likes, and comments on your social media posts

Key Takeaways

Developing a social media plan for events is crucial to ensure that your social media efforts are aligned with your overall event marketing strategy. It is important to set specific goals, identify your target audience, choose the right social media platforms, create an engaging content plan, and promote your event on social media to drive ticket sales. Encouraging attendees to engage with your event on social media and leveraging user-generated content to showcase your event can help generate buzz and engagement. Finally, tracking and analyzing the impact of your social media efforts on event success is crucial to understanding the effectiveness of your social media plan.

CHAPTER 15: CREATING A SOCIAL MEDIA STRATEGY FOR NONPROFITS

Nonprofit organizations have a unique set of challenges when it comes to social media strategy. Unlike businesses, their focus is more on raising awareness and funding than selling products or services. In this chapter, we will discuss how nonprofits can create an effective social media presence that engages supporters, promotes their cause, and maximizes fundraising efforts.

Understanding the Unique Challenges of Nonprofit Social Media

Nonprofits face several challenges when it comes to social media, primarily due to their limited resources compared to businesses. They often operate on shoestring budgets and rely heavily on volunteers, which can make it challenging to develop and execute a comprehensive social media strategy. Additionally, nonprofits typically have a broader audience compared to businesses, which means they need to tailor their messaging to different segments.

Creating a Social Media Plan for Nonprofits

To create an effective social media plan, nonprofits need to establish clear goals and objectives. Some common goals for nonprofits include raising awareness, engaging supporters, increasing donations, recruiting volunteers, and building partnerships. Once the goals have been set, nonprofits should choose the social media platforms that are most relevant to their target audience. Facebook, Twitter, and Instagram are popular choices for nonprofits, but they should also consider LinkedIn, YouTube, and other platforms depending on their objectives.

Maximizing Fundraising Efforts through Social Media

Social media can be a powerful tool for nonprofits to raise funds and donations. Some ways nonprofits can leverage social media to maximize their fundraising efforts include:

❖ Crowdfunding: Nonprofits can use crowdfunding platforms like Kickstarter, Indiegogo, and GoFundMe to raise funds for specific campaigns or projects.

❖ Online donation pages: Nonprofits should make it easy for supporters to donate through their website and social media channels by providing a secure online donation page.

❖ Peer-to-peer fundraising: Nonprofits can tap into the networks of their supporters and launch peer-to-peer fundraising campaigns, where supporters create their fundraising pages on behalf of the nonprofit.

Engaging Volunteers and Donors on Social Media

Nonprofits can also use social media to engage their supporters and donors, creating a sense of community and loyalty. This can be achieved through a variety of tactics, including:

❖ Live streaming: Nonprofits can use platforms such as Facebook Live or Instagram Live to showcase events, highlight initiatives, and engage with their supporters in real-time.

❖ Advocacy campaigns: Social media can be used to launch advocacy campaigns that encourage supporters to take action on issues related to the nonprofit's mission.

❖ User-generated content: Nonprofits can engage their supporters by soliciting user-generated content, such as photos or videos related to their cause.

Measuring the Impact of Social Media on Nonprofit Success

Measuring the impact of social media on nonprofit success should go beyond just counting the number of followers or likes. Nonprofits should identify key performance indicators (KPIs) that align with their goals and objectives, such as the amount of money raised, the number of volunteers recruited, or the reach of their campaigns. Social media analytics tools such as Google Analytics and Hootsuite Insights can provide valuable insights into which social media channels are driving engagement and conversions.

Overcoming Common Challenges in Nonprofit Social Media

Nonprofits face several challenges when it comes to social media, but some of the most common ones include limited resources, lack of expertise, and the difficulty of measuring the impact of social media on their goals. To overcome these challenges, nonprofits should consider partnering with social media experts, leveraging volunteers and other resources, and focusing on specific goals and objectives that can be easily measured.

Key Takeaways

❖ Nonprofit organizations face unique challenges when it comes to social media strategy, including limited resources and a broad audience.

❖ To create an effective social media plan, nonprofits should establish clear goals and objectives, choose relevant social media channels, and tailor their messaging to different segments.

❖ Social media can be an effective tool for nonprofits to raise funds and donations, engage their volunteers and donors, and create a sense of community and loyalty.

❖ Measuring the impact of social media on nonprofit success should go beyond the number of followers or likes, and instead focus on key performance indicators (KPIs) that align with their goals and objectives.

❖ To overcome common challenges in nonprofit social media, nonprofits should consider partnering with social media experts, leveraging volunteers and other resources, and focusing on specific goals and objectives that can be easily measured.

CHAPTER 16: MANAGING MULTIPLE SOCIAL MEDIA ACCOUNTS

Most businesses find it necessary to have a presence on multiple social media platforms to reach their target audience and grow their brand. While having multiple social media accounts can be beneficial for a business, it can also present challenges in managing and coordinating content across platforms. In this chapter, we will explore how to effectively manage multiple social media accounts to ensure a consistent and cohesive brand message.

Understanding the Challenges

Managing multiple social media accounts can be overwhelming, especially for small businesses or organizations with limited resources. It requires time, effort, and careful planning to ensure that each platform is being used strategically and that messaging remains consistent across all accounts. Some of the common challenges that businesses face when managing multiple social media accounts include:

❖ Time constraints: Maintaining multiple social media accounts requires a significant amount of time and effort.

Business owners and employees are often stretched thin, and it can be challenging to find the time to create and post content on all accounts consistently.

❖ Content creation: Each social media platform has unique requirements for the types of content that perform well. For example, Instagram is image-focused, while Twitter is text-heavy. Creating content that is tailored to each platform can be time-consuming and requires a degree of creativity.

❖ Keeping messaging consistent: A business's social media presence should be consistent across all platforms to maintain a unified brand message. However, it can be difficult to maintain consistency when managing multiple accounts.

❖ Coordinating efforts: If multiple employees are responsible for managing social media accounts, it can be challenging to coordinate efforts and ensure everyone is on the same page.

Creating Processes for Managing Multiple Social Media Accounts

To effectively manage multiple social media accounts, it's essential to create a process for how content is created, approved, and posted. The first step in developing a process is to identify the employees responsible for managing each account. Assigning responsibility ensures that there is accountability, and each platform receives the attention it deserves.

Next, it's crucial to create a content calendar that outlines what type of content will be posted on each platform. The calendar should include publishing dates and times, ensuring that content is posted regularly across all accounts. A content calendar also helps ensure that messaging remains consistent and avoids duplicating content across platforms.

Leveraging Social Media Management Tools

Using social media management tools can simplify the process of managing multiple social media accounts. Many tools, such as Hootsuite or Sprout Social, allow businesses to manage and track their social media accounts from one central location. These tools can help save time by allowing businesses to create and schedule posts across all platforms simultaneously. They also provide analytics and reports to track performance and engagement on each platform, providing valuable insights into the effectiveness of content.

Coordinating Social Media Efforts Across Teams and Departments

Effective coordination and communication are critical for managing multiple social media accounts. If multiple employees or teams are responsible for managing accounts, it's essential to establish a plan to coordinate efforts and ensure everyone is aligned. Establishing a process for content approval and review can help keep messaging consistent and ensure that everyone is working towards the same social media goals.

Measuring the Effectiveness of Social Media Management

To determine the effectiveness of managing multiple social media accounts, it's essential to measure the engagement and impact of each account. Analytics tools provided by social media platforms, as well as social media management tools, can provide valuable insights into the performance of each account. Utilizing these insights to optimize and adjust content can help improve engagement and drive business results.

Best Practices for Managing Multiple Social Media Accounts

To effectively manage multiple social media accounts, here are some best practices to consider:

❖ Assign responsibility and establish processes: Ensure that each platform has an owner, and establish a process for creating, approving, and posting content.

❖ Create a content calendar: Develop a content calendar to ensure each account is updated regularly and that messaging remains consistent.

❖ Leverage social media management tools: Use social media management tools to streamline the process of managing multiple accounts.

❖ Coordinating social media efforts: Establish a plan for coordinating efforts between teams and departments to ensure messaging remains consistent.

Conclusion

Managing multiple social media accounts can be challenging, but with the right processes, tools, and coordination, it can be an effective way to reach a broader audience and grow your business. By creating a content calendar, leveraging social media management tools, and coordinating efforts across teams and departments, businesses can effectively manage their social media accounts and provide a consistent and cohesive brand message across all platforms.

CHAPTER 17: DEVELOPING A SOCIAL MEDIA STRATEGY FOR E-COMMERCE

Social media has become an integral part of an e-commerce business's marketing strategy. Through social media platforms, businesses can connect with potential customers, build brand loyalty, and increase sales.

However, developing a successful social media strategy for e-commerce can be challenging. In this chapter, we will explore the key elements of a social media strategy for e-commerce businesses, common challenges, and best practices to maximize your success on social media.

Understanding the Role of Social Media in E-commerce

As an e-commerce business, your social media strategy should aim to drive traffic to your website, increase conversions, and grow your customer base. By leveraging social media channels, you can reach a wider audience, build brand awareness, and foster a community of loyal customers.

To develop a successful social media strategy for your e-commerce business, you need to identify the social media channels that are most relevant to your target audience. For example, if you are targeting a younger demographic, you may want to focus on platforms like Instagram and Snapchat, while a B2B e-commerce business may want to focus on LinkedIn.

It's also important to have a clear understanding of your audience's social media behavior. What times of day are they most active on social media? What types of content do they engage with the most? By analyzing this data, you can optimize your social media content to better resonate with your audience.

Creating a Social Media Plan for E-commerce

A social media plan is essential for any successful e-commerce social media strategy. Your plan should outline your social media goals, target audience, content strategy, and metrics you will use to measure success.

One key element of an e-commerce social media plan is a content calendar. A content calendar is a schedule of the content you plan to publish on your social media channels. A well-planned content calendar ensures that your social media content is consistent, relevant to your audience, and promotes your products effectively.

To drive sales through social media, you need to create a balance of promotional and non-promotional content. Your promotional content should highlight your products' unique features and benefits and encourage your audience to take action, such as making a purchase or signing up for your email list. Non-promotional content can include user-generated content, behind-the-scenes content, and educational content related to your products or industry.

Maximizing Sales Through Social Media Channels

To maximize your e-commerce business's sales through social media, you must optimize your social media channels for conversion. This means creating an easy-to-use social media shopping experience that guides your audience towards making a purchase.

One effective way to optimize your social media channels for conversion is by using shoppable posts. Shoppable posts allow you to tag your products directly within an image and include a link to purchase. This makes it easy for your audience to shop your products directly from your social media channels.

You can also incorporate user-generated content into your social media strategy to drive sales. User-generated content, such as customer photos of your products, can be very effective in promoting your brand and driving conversions. By leveraging user-generated content, you can showcase your products in an authentic and relatable way that resonates with potential customers.

Measuring the Impact of Social Media on E-commerce Success

Measuring the effectiveness of your social media strategy is essential for understanding what is working and what needs improvement. By tracking the right metrics, you can gauge the impact of your social media efforts on your e-commerce business's success.

Some key metrics to track for e-commerce businesses include conversion rate, click-through rate, and average order value. Conversion rate measures the percentage of visitors to your site who make a purchase. Click-through rate measures the percentage of clicks on your social media posts that lead to your website. Average order value measures the average value of each purchase made on your website.

By analyzing these metrics, you can optimize your social media strategy to better align with your e-commerce business's goals.

Overcoming Common Challenges in E-commerce Social Media

Like any social media strategy, e-commerce businesses face common challenges such as managing multiple social media channels, creating engaging content, and measuring ROI.

One of the biggest challenges for e-commerce businesses is managing their reputation on social media. Negative feedback or reviews on social media can spread quickly and damage your brand's reputation. To mitigate this risk, it's essential to stay on top of your social media channels, respond to feedback quickly and professionally, and develop a crisis management plan for social media.

Another challenge e-commerce businesses face is standing out from the competition. With so many brands competing for attention on social media, it's essential to develop a unique brand voice, create visually appealing content, and offer promotions or discounts that differentiate your brand.

Key Takeaways

In conclusion, developing a successful social media strategy for your e-commerce business requires careful planning, optimization, and measurement. By focusing on your audience's social media behavior, creating engaging content, optimizing your social media channels for conversion, measuring the impact of your social media efforts, and overcoming common challenges, you can increase brand awareness, drive sales, and grow your e-commerce business through social media channels.

CHAPTER 18: CREATING A SOCIAL MEDIA STRATEGY FOR B2B COMPANIES

B2B companies have traditionally focused on traditional marketing methods like trade shows, conferences, and print advertising. However, with the rise of social media, it has become essential for B2B companies to have a strong social media presence. In this chapter, we will discuss the unique challenges of creating a social media strategy for B2B companies and provide actionable tips for developing a successful strategy.

Understanding the Unique Challenges of B2B Social Media

The B2B sales cycle is notoriously long and complex, which can make it challenging to create effective social media strategies. Additionally, the B2B decision-making process often involves multiple stakeholders, which adds further complexity to social media efforts. Here are some unique challenges that B2B companies face when creating a social media strategy:

❖ Reaching Decision Makers: Unlike in B2C marketing, where the target audience is relatively broad, B2B companies typically have a specific group of decision-makers they need to target. Reaching this group can be challenging, as decision-makers are often difficult to reach.

❖   Limited Content: B2B companies may struggle to create compelling content that's relevant to their industry. Unlike consumer-facing companies, the content produced by B2B companies may be more technical and niche. B2B companies must find ways to make their content engaging and compelling to their target audience.

❖   Measuring ROI: B2B sales cycles can be long and complex, making it difficult to measure the impact of social media marketing efforts on the bottom line. B2B companies must find ways to track ROI effectively to justify social media investments.

Creating a Social Media Plan for B2B Companies

Despite these challenges, B2B companies can develop effective social media strategies to engage decision-makers, build relationships, and drive leads. Here are some tips for creating a social media plan for a B2B company:

❖   Identify Your Target Audience: To be successful on social media, B2B companies need to understand their target audience and what motivates them. Definition of a target audience involves considering several factors, including what type of companies they work for, what their job title is, what industry they are in, and what their pain points are.

❖   Choose the Right Platforms: Not every social media platform is appropriate for B2B companies. LinkedIn is an obvious choice for B2B companies, as it is a professional networking site that attracts decision-makers. In addition, Twitter can be a great platform for B2B companies to share industry news and updates.

❖   Produce Relevant Content: Creating valuable and informative content that is targeted towards B2B decision-makers is essential for building engagement and generating leads. Content should be educational, informative, and aim to solve the problems or answer the questions your target audience has.

❖ Leverage Influencers: Influencer marketing, if done right, can be extremely effective for B2B companies. Find thought leaders in your industry who have a strong social media presence and who would be a good fit to collaborate with your brand.

❖ Join Conversations: By responding to people on social media and engaging in conversations and discussions relevant to your industry, you can build trust and position yourself as an authority.

❖ Track and Analyze Metrics: Tracking the right metrics is important to show the ROI of your social media efforts and improving the effectiveness of future campaigns. Metrics that B2B companies should focus on include conversions, reach, engagement, and sentiment.

Overcoming Common Challenges in B2B Social Media

Here are some common challenges that B2B companies face while implementing a social media strategy and ways to overcome them:

❖ Limited Resources: B2B companies may not have large marketing teams or budgets. However, by focusing on fewer platforms and creating high-quality, targeted content, B2B companies can make the most of their limited resources.

❖ Lack of Time: Social media can be time-consuming for B2B companies who may be juggling multiple other responsibilities. Creating a social media content calendar can help to streamline the process, making it easier to create and publish content regularly.

❖   Decision Maker Participation: It is not uncommon for decision-makers to shy away from social media for fear of negative comments or losing control of messaging. However, having decision-makers involved and active on social media can help to humanize a brand and build trust.

Key Takeaways

A successful social media strategy for B2B companies involves targeting the right audience, creating targeted content, choosing the right platforms, leveraging influencers, joining conversations, and measuring the right metrics. Despite the challenges, social media is a critical part of the marketing mix for B2B companies. Understanding the unique needs of the industry will better position B2B companies to create effective social media strategies.

CHAPTER 19: CREATING A SUCCESSFUL EMPLOYEE BRANDING STRATEGY ON SOCIAL MEDIA

Employee branding on social media is a powerful tool for businesses to promote their brand and culture. Employees can act as brand ambassadors and share the company's values and vision with their social media networks, increasing the brand's reach and credibility. Moreover, active participation in social media by employees can help businesses attract and retain top talent, improve employee morale, and create a positive work environment. Therefore, it is essential for businesses to create a successful employee branding strategy on social media.

Understanding Employee Branding on Social Media

Employee branding is the practice of promoting a company's brand and values through employee advocacy and social media marketing. Employee branding is based on the belief that happy and engaged employees are more likely to share positive experiences about their workplace on social media, which in turn, can increase brand visibility and attract customers and job candidates. Employee branding can also ensure that employees feel connected to the company's values and missions, leading to a more motivated and productive workforce.

Creating an Employee Branding Strategy on Social Media

A successful employee branding strategy on social media requires a company to empower its employees to participate in social media marketing. Here are the essential steps to create an effective employee branding program:

❖ Train and Educate Employees: To participate in social media marketing, employees need to be trained and informed about the company's branding guidelines, social media policies, and best practices for social media marketing. A company must ensure that employees are aware and understand the do's and don'ts of social media marketing to maintain a consistent branding message and avoid reputational risks.

❖ Encourage Employee Participation: Employees should be encouraged to participate in social media marketing by sharing their positive experiences about the company on social media platforms. Additionally, businesses can offer incentives to employees who participate in social media marketing initiatives like discounts, rewards, or recognition programs for their contributions to the company's branding efforts.

❖ Provide Content and Resources: Providing employees with pre-approved content, such as blog posts, infographics, and videos, can make it easy for them to share professional content on social media platforms. It can also save them time and effort, making it more likely that they will participate in social media marketing. Moreover, companies can provide training and resources to employees on how to create engaging content, take and post quality photos, and develop strong social media campaigns.

❖ Monitor and Measure Employee Branding: Monitoring social media activities and measuring the success of employee branding programs is essential to assess the impact of the branding efforts on the company. Companies must track employee engagement rates, follower counts, and social media analytics to determine the overall success of social media marketing campaigns.

Best Practices for Employee Branding on Social Media

Here are some best practices for creating a successful employee branding strategy on social media:

❖ Build Trust: Trust is critical when it comes to employee branding on social media. Companies must build trust with their employees by creating an open and supportive work environment that values employee input and encourages transparency. Employees need to feel comfortable sharing their experiences on social media platforms.

❖ Keep Messaging Consistent: Consistency is key when it comes to branding messaging. Employers must ensure that their messaging on social media platforms is consistent with the branding and communications message they want to convey to their customers.

❖ Develop a Social Media Policy: Creating a social media policy can provide employees with clear guidelines on acceptable social media behavior, including what types of content they can share about the company and its products/services.

❖ Encourage Diversity: Companies must encourage and embrace diversity in their social media branding efforts. Highlight employees from different backgrounds, experiences, and perspectives to promote diversity and inclusivity.

Overcoming Common Challenges in Employee Branding on Social Media

Despite the benefits of employee branding on social media, there are several common challenges that employers may encounter when implementing employee branding initiatives. Here are three of the most common challenges and strategies for overcoming them:

❖ Ensuring Consistency: Consistency can be challenging, especially when dealing with a large employee base. Therefore, it is essential to develop clear branding guidelines to help employees understand their role in social media branding initiatives.

❖ Dealing with Negative Feedback: Negative feedback on social media can be inevitable and sometimes harmful to a company's reputation. Employers should work with employees to address negative feedback and develop strategies to minimize potential negative impacts.

❖ Preventing Legal Risks: Companies must ensure that employee social media posts are compliant with legal requirements, including content usage, data privacy, and employment laws. Employers should monitor and review employee social media posts regularly to ensure that they are in compliance with legal requirements.

Key Takeaways

Employee branding on social media is a valuable tool for companies to promote their brand and engage employees in social media marketing. Creating an effective employee branding strategy involves training and educating employees on social media policies, encouraging employee participation, providing content and resources, monitoring and measuring employee branding performance, adhering to best practices, and overcoming common challenges. A successful employee branding strategy can increase brand reach, improve employee morale and retention, and create a positive work environment.

CHAPTER 20: THE FUTURE OF SOCIAL MEDIA STRATEGY

Social media has grown at an unprecedented rate and transformed the way businesses interact with their clients and customers. As a result, businesses must stay ahead of emerging trends and technologies to leverage them to the fullest. In the same manner, the future of social media strategy depends on how businesses adapt to these next steps.

Predictions for the Future of Social Media

Several experts have predicted the future of social media, and some speculate that the industry may only be in its early stages of growth. Here are some of the predictions that businesses must keep in mind:

❖ AR and VR will become mainstream: Augmented reality (AR) and virtual reality (VR) have been on the rise in the past years, and they will become more common in the coming years. AR and VR will allow businesses to create immersive experiences for their customers, and this would impact social media platforms as well.

❖ Short-form video will dominate: Short-form video, such as videos on TikTok and Instagram Stories, has gained immense popularity in recent years. The demand for short-form video content will continue to rise, and businesses must adapt to this style of content creation.

❖ AI and chatbots will shape communication: AI and chatbots have made significant advances in communication and customer service. The use of chatbots will increase in the future, and businesses must implement these technologies to improve customer service.

❖ Social media commerce will gain momentum: Social commerce, the process of buying and selling products directly from social media platforms, has already taken off in some areas. It is predicted that this trend will continue to grow, and businesses must be prepared to implement social commerce strategies.

Incorporating Emerging Technologies into your Social Media Strategy

As emerging technologies become more common, businesses must learn to integrate them into their social media strategies. One example is the integration of AI and chatbots into social media customer service. The use of chatbots can improve response times and make customer service more efficient.

AR and VR can be utilized to create engaging content and allow customers to experience products and services in a more immersive way. Short-form video can also be easily integrated into social media strategies to create compelling content that resonates with audiences.

Preparing for the Next Wave of Social Media Trends

It's important to stay ahead of the curve when it comes to social media trends and technologies. Keeping up-to-date with the latest industry thought leaders, reading reports, and attending conferences on social media is crucial for businesses that aim to stay ahead of the competition.

However, many businesses may fall into the trap of over-focusing on new platforms while disregarding established ones. The most critical task is adapting to changes, but with the understanding that established platforms still offer value, businesses should be flexible enough to adjust their strategies for each platform.

Overcoming Challenges in Adapting to New Social Media Platforms

One of the challenges of adapting to new technologies is remaining flexible enough to avoid missing out on exciting new opportunities. A significant impediment to the growth of any business is an inability to adapt to changes as rapidly as the market demands.

Early movers for social media platforms tend to achieve the maximum benefit, even if there is a considerable risk of jumping in too soon. By ensuring that a business is on the cutting edge of digital marketing strategies, any business could take advantage of the first follower effect and get ahead of competitors.

Best Practices for Staying Ahead of Social Media Changes

Staying ahead of the social media trends requires constant effort and a commitment to remaining updated on the latest industry insights. Here are some best practices to stay ahead of the curve:

- ❖ Attend industry conferences: Attend social media conferences and other marketing events to keep up with the latest trends and innovations.

- ❖ Follow industry thought leaders: Learn from established experts in the field by following thought leaders across social media platforms.

- ❖ Continuously monitor social media trends: Monitor social media trends by conducting regular research and analysis on the ever-evolving social media landscape.

❖ Experiment and take risks: Experiment with new social media strategies and take intelligent risks to find new and innovative ways to engage with customers.

❖ Seek out younger employees: Hire younger employees who have grown up immersed in social media culture to stay up-to-date on emerging trends and be open to new ideas.

Key Takeaways

Social media is an ever-changing ecosystem, and businesses must stay ahead of emerging trends, technologies, and platforms to maximize their return on investment. Incorporating new technologies, such as AR, VR, chatbots, and AI, and staying updated on the latest industry thought leaders and trends, are essential for businesses to remain successful in their social media strategies.

Continuously monitoring social media trends and experimenting with new social media strategies is vital to improve customer engagement and stay competitive. Businesses should embrace a proactive approach in adapting to social media changes and remain inquisitive enough to try new strategies that could help them stand out from their competition.

By keeping these strategies in mind and adapting early on, businesses can leverage new technologies and remain competitive in their social media strategies for years to come.

Final Thoughts

As we come to the end of this book, I hope you have gained valuable insight into the world of social media and how it can be used to build a successful business. Remember, social media is not just about posting pretty pictures or sharing funny memes. It's about creating a community that engages with your brand and fosters trust.

Creating a strong social media strategy takes time and effort, but it's worth it in the long run. You have the power to reach millions of potential customers through these platforms, so use them wisely.

Remember to constantly evaluate your strategy, analyze your metrics, and adjust accordingly. Social media is constantly evolving, so don't be afraid to try out new tactics and experiment with different approaches.

The key is to always prioritize quality over quantity. Don't simply post for the sake of posting; make sure each piece of content serves a purpose and aligns with your overall brand message.

And finally, don't forget that behind every screen is a real person. Treat your followers with kindness and respect, and always strive to provide them with value.

Thank you for joining me on this journey towards mastering social media strategy. Now get out there and start building your online empire!

ABOUT THE AUTHOR

Ray Goodwin

Ray Goodwin, is the author behind this series of captivating books on Business Development and self improvement, and has left an indelible mark on the field. He was born and raised in the bustling city of London, where he developed a strong work ethic and an insatiable curiosity about the inner workings of successful businesses. Throughout his illustrious career, Ray leveraged his extensive knowledge and experience to help numerous companies flourish and prosper.

His keen insights and innovative strategies has earned him recognition, driving him to share his expertise with others. Ray believes in the power of sharing knowledge to elevate businesses and empower aspiring entrepreneurs.

Ray's dedication to his craft is evident in the numerous books he has authored on business development and self improvement. His writing style seamlessly blends practical advice, thought-provoking concepts, and real-life case studies, making his books invaluable resources for business professionals and novices alike. His ability to distill complex concepts into accessible language has greatly impacted the lives and careers of countless individuals.

Now retired from the corporate world, Ray and his beloved wife have settled in the idyllic English countryside. Surrounded by the beauty of nature, Ray finds inspiration for his writing and indulges in his hobbies.

Ray Goodwin's books continue to serve as enduring guides for those seeking success in the business world. With a wealth of experience and a deep understanding of the inner workings of businesses, Ray's work remains a testament to his passion for sharing knowledge and helping others flourish.

www.ingramcontent.com/pod-product-compliance
Lightning Source LLC
Chambersburg PA
CBHW062353290526
45794CB00005B/2202